melancholy occurrence

Also by John Seed

Spaces In (Pig Press, Newcastle-upon Tyne 1977)

History Labour Night (Pig Press, Durham 1984)

Interior in the Open Air (Reality Studios, London 1993)

Divided into One (Poetical Histories, Cambridge 2003)

New and Collected Poems (Shearsman Books, Exeter 2005)

Pictures from Mayhew (Shearsman Books, Exeter 2005)

That Barrikins (Shearsman Books, Exeter 2007)

Manchester: August 16th & 17th 1819 (Intercapillary Editions, London 2013)

Some Poems, 2006-12 (Gratton Street Irregulars, Cheltenham, 2014)

Smoke Rising (Shearsman Books, Bristol, 2015)

Brandon Pithouse. Recollections of the Durham Coalfield (Smokestack Books, Ripon, 2016)

John Seed

melancholy occurrence

Shearsman Books

First published in the United Kingdom in 2018 by
Shearsman Books
50 Westons Hill Drive
Emersons Green
BRISTOL
BS16 7DF

Shearsman Books Ltd Registered Office
30–31 St. James Place, Mangotsfield, Bristol BS16 9JB
(this address not for correspondence)

www.shearsman.com

ISBN 978-1-84861-581-6

These pieces are appropriated from mostly nineteenth-century
English newspapers or inquest reports and rewritten. Without
changing significant details. They are not fiction therefore any
relation to persons living or dead is not entirely coincidental.

A handful have already appeared in
*Tears in the Fence, Poetry Salzburg Review, Card Alpha,
First Offense, Ink Sweat and Tears,* and *nonsite.org.*

Weight, pressure, and accidental movement together with resistance are the four accidental powers in which all the visible works of mortals have their existence and their end.

—Leonardo da Vinci
quoted by Edward Robert Zurko,
Origins of Functionalist Theory, (New York, 1957), p.53.

'One always fails to speak of what one loves'

on blank paper Barthes left

in his typewriter the Monday morning he

stepped off the curb at 44 Rue des Écoles

ronron the drone of traffic

art of the contingent   there's always something else

something about the sky the cold the winter light

and was hit by a laundry van one afternoon

25 February 1980

Sunday 26th December

1820 London

in French-alley Goswell-street

the watchman going his rounds

calling the hour of one

discovered a new-born infant

lying in a corner entirely naked

a few old rags around his head

About six o'clock Saturday evening

18th May 1850

a man staggered down High Street Glasgow

reached North Gray's Close

and fell down

and died in the infirmary a few hours later his

name is unknown

his dress that of a labourer

A stonemason died a short time since at Woolwich

employed three years making his own brick grave
and erecting his own tombstone

he carried the work on to the finishing
of the inscription leaving only

a blank for the date

About three o'clock

Monday October 31st 1814

south-west corner of the Bank

one of the figures

dropped onto the head of a passer-by

who had just received a dividend

killing him and leaving a fracture

almost an inch wide

visible in the west wall

Edward Charles Luard

of Jesus College Cambridge

wishing to see some friends

at Southampton

leaving for Jersey from the end of the pier

midnight Wednesday 28th June 1854

making haste in the darkness

being short-sighted he

fell over the quay

wall into the water

and disappeared

Henry Farley a very quiet man   having little to say

got out of bed about half past five

in the open door of an outhouse at the back of his cottage got up

on a four-inch set-off in the brickwork   then slipped off

a widower aged 67 suffering from rheumatism   a shepherd out of

work   and given notice to leave his cottage at Upper Woodford

by Michaelmas

hanging from a beam his feet scarcely an inch from the ground

Sunday morning going over his farm

Mr Way noticed the tools and coat of a labourer named Tremlett

employed the previous day

10th of November 1877

to level a cob-wall

his body buried beneath the ruins

pocket watch stopped at two minutes to four o'clock

Jennings an illusionist

and conjuror at the Royal Aquarium

entered a butcher's shop on the Fulham Road

and fell through an open trap-door

During the rejoicings Thursday evening

5 November 1807

somebody discharged a musket behind the watch-house

the ball passed through window shutters

on each side of the watch-house

and through the head of Sarah Osborne

fourteen years of age

standing in a shop in Bristol's Horse Fair

then through the windows of the house opposite

shattering a picture on the wall

Mrs Mary Rothes a pew-opener

performing her duties during morning service at Cripplegate

Sunday 8th of February 1835

fell suddenly to the ground saying

O god have mercy on me

and before anybody could reach her

ceased to exist

private of the 14th Regiment

Charles Sturges

aged twenty-four

shot himself through the heart

at four in the morning

Tuesday 10 May 1876

on sentry at the barracks

Plymouth

in the dressing room at the Victoria Skating Rink

Friday December 2nd 1910

William Lewis of Druid's Lodge

dressed as an arctic explorer

head to foot in cotton wool

lit a cigarette

next minute a flash

a sheet of flame

rushed out of the room

Agnes Harriet Gilman aged three years

a winter night Friday about five

stepped into Ashborne-road Derby

and onto the tramway

and turned and ran

straight towards the car the horse

knocked her down across the rail

it was dark

the red lights of the car threw no light on the track

and the child was very little

and dressed in dark clothes

and the wheels went over her

folded up near the flood-gates

end of the Mill-pond by the path

from the Castle Green to the Infirmary

two servants discovered the cloak and bonnet of Mary Ridler

and then her body

drowned in the Castle Mill-pond

close to the same gates she was

about thirty years of age

sitting on the pavement unconscious

leaning against one of the houses

Halket-street Canton in Cardiff

seven o'clock on the morning of Christmas Day

1891

he never regained consciousness and could not be identified

he died of chronic bronchitis hastened by exposure

2d in his pocket

Friday 13th

September 1889

in Cooper's warehouse in Glasgow

a boy named Alexander McKay

swung a rope around his neck

in frolic one end

caught in a shaft drives the belting overhead

and he was dragged up

and strangled

Robert Baker of Kingsteignton

in charge of a horse

drawing stones from the quarry to

the kiln-bed at Harcombe Lime-kilns

backed the cart against the pit circle

placing a ten-foot pole behind the wheels

as the stone was tipped horse and cart

fell back into the burning pit and

trying to free the horse from its harness he

suffocated in the fumes of burning lime

During a tremendous thunderstorm

Sunday se'en night August 1811

at South Park near Hedon

in the parlour after supper

sitting with his head close to the bell handle

Mr Robinson was instantly struck dead

a small discoloured place on one side of his neck

one on his thigh but no other

marks of the stroke

were visible

pumping hot liquor out of a mash tub

back of the Bay Horse Inn

North-road Preston

Monday afternoon December 14th 1863

William Moss

slipped off the stage and falling

head first into the mash tub

was scalded to death

Caroline Pedder

wife of James Pedder a tailor

of Albert-place in Putney

about noon preparing dinner

sparks from burning wood

touched her dress unnoticed until

at the corner of the street

entering Woodlands the grocers she

burst into flames

on Monday 23rd April 1849

about two o'clock

shortly after the patients had dined

Charles Pile aged 34

hanged himself by his neckerchief

to the bracket of the roller of the towel-runner

in the general washing room of the ward

at the Devon County Pauper Lunatic Asylum Exminster

On Saturday 11th August 1764

two brick-makers

drank three quarts of cherry-brandy

in Gray's-inn-lane

for a trifling wager

one of them named Spawton expired a few hours after

and the other named Langton 'tis thought

cannot survive

during the storm at Pinhoe

October 1877

twenty minutes after eleven at night

a tall chimney crashed through the length of the roof

of the Post Office

leaving nothing but two or three feet of slating at the end

and burying under fallen debris

Miss Elizabeth Bambury aged 53

crushed to death in a stooping posture

as she was unfastening her boots

some hours tracing a fox in the snow

destroying it around midday

and then at the houses of neighbours

liberally supplied with beer and cider

William Jackman a farmer's son aged 16 years

was much intoxicated by 7 o'clock

without his hat rambling

towards his home quarter of a mile away

and the next morning at daybreak

discovered lying by the side of the road

frozen to death

a hundred yards from his Father's house

the death of Robert Hitt

aged 22

shoemaker at Otterton

February 1827

from a blow

falling on his

head running to

pick up his

hat blown off

by the wind

after breakfast she retired

into a little armoury of her father's

like the guard room of St. James's

walls decorated with swords pistols

and shot herself below the breast

aiming at her heart and missing she

lived a quarter of an hour

she was sixteen

body partly on the

pavement partly on the road blood

streaming from the back of his head

Cornelius Grinnell of New York

owner of the steam yacht *Hawk*

lodging at the Royal Victoria Yacht Club

on Pier Street in Ryde

returning to his rooms after midnight

drew up the Venetian blinds

opened the window and stepped out

onto a balcony that wasn't there

and disappeared

a Saturday evening April 1906

four men in a trap

riding from Oldham towards Ripponden

from a culvert sheep

ran in front of the horse

took fright and backed the carriage

through a wall and over a cliff

dropping ninety feet into the quarry at Derby Delph

killing three of them

George Seed

crawled out of the wreckage

Archduchess Matilda

scion of the house of Hapsburg-Lorraine

intended wife of

Humbert Prince of Piedmont heir to the Italian throne

a princess in her nineteenth year she died she

trod on a Lucifer match

on a summer morning

as she leaned out of the window

and her summer dress was instantly ablaze

the horn was blown

Exeter at 5 o'clock the *Defiance* coach

passing through knocked him down

incautiously driving a wheel-barrow in the middle of the road

Samuel Coggen 77 years of age

deaf imperfect eyesight

up a very badly lighted Paris-street

alighting from a moving omnibus

heading along Goldhawk Road

as it passed the railway bridge

Robert Bowman Diack

lost his balance and

struggling to obtain his perpendicular

fell across the road

was kicked by horses of the omnibus following

and the wheels passed over him

first day at work aged fourteen

Sharp's Saw Mills at St. Thomas

standing on the iron table

stooping to remove a piece of wood

his foot slipped and he fell

on to the saw his right leg

was cut off just below the knee

both arms were mutilated jagged and torn

a wound across the face almost dividing the head

he breathed two or three times

Three female children

going along Mosley Street Newcastle-upon-Tyne

the eldest aged 11

picked up a paper with something enclosed

gave a small portion to her sisters

and ate the rest herself

taken extremely ill

she died in great agony the

following day the

others were saved

William Shapland

labourer aged 61

without constant employment

or fixed home

and a great abhorrence of the workhouse

living partly on charity

and sleeping about in stables and outhouses

was found dead February 1848

in a hay-loft in Hole Water

riding together on a horse

towards Launceston

Carlyon's hat falling into the road

Thomas Robins eighteen years of age

riding behind

carrying in his right hand a loaded percussion gun

drew the ramrod

and endeavouring to reach the hat

the gun went off

and the whole load entered under his right ear

Friday afternoon 15th of May

1896 cycling in Smith

Street Warwick the Countess

avoiding a passing vehicle

in the narrow thoroughfare

ran full tilt into

the Earl of Warwick

walking in the roadway

knocking him over but

fortunately keeping her seat

Sunday a summer night

James Brookbank pianoforte maker

jumped out of a railway carriage at Shoreditch

before the train was at rest

and falling between carriage and platform

was squeezed to death against the abutment

returning home from Exeter at St. David's Station

a few minutes after four

Friday afternoon

carrying with him a sack

a barrel of yeast weighing 36 lbs

purchased at the City Brewery

William Richards

mounted the stone steps

crossing the bridge to the North Devon platform

the barrel in the sack on his right shoulder

was seen to lurch over

and not releasing his hold

he was pulled over the balustrade

pitching on to the stone platform eleven feet below

fracturing his spine

A scaffolder Henry Clemson

Park Street Barnsbury

Thursday evening

September 1896

fell forty feet

from a scaffold

on top of a passer-by

a woman

Saturday night August 31st 1816

doing some plastering

in the Dublin brewery of Messrs Connolly and Somers

James Keenan aged 14

crossing a plank above a large vat

130 hogsheads of porter

missed his step

fell into the foaming gulph and

suffocated

the plate he was standing on

a half-inch thick

fractured

and he was standing in

scalding water a foot deep

at the Duffryn Tin-plate Works

Morriston

6th January 1910

A cornfactor named Turk

speculating largely in corn

hanged himself in a stable at

South Cave East Riding

July 1801

driven to suicide by

the uncommon promise

of the coming harvest

Benjamin Colley aged 61

a charcoal burner

living in the woods

near West Anstey

ill with pneumonia

sleeping out nights

allowed shelter

in a loft over a henhouse

behind the *Partridge Arms*

died a few days later

on the road

to the Union workhouse

thrown from a pony

his feet entangled in the stirrups

George Cousins aged 15

was dragged at full speed

for nearly half a mile along the road

taken up senseless at Spreyton he

lived but a few hours

and reaching out for the handle

missed it slipped

falling back on his left shoulder

when he rushed into Okehampton station

made a jump at the door of a third class carriage

Walter J. Palmer veterinary surgeon

42 years of age in July 1896

and tumbled in between two coaches his head

was nearly severed from the trunk

as the 11.43 train was leaving

telegram in his pocket

4th May 1804

Westover house near Bath damaged by lightning an explosion
louder than any cannon

The wainscot was burned the bells were melted the door-post split to
pieces

In one chamber all but three window panes were broken looking
glass shivered to pieces wainscoting torn away and driven through
the bed curtains

Every bason wine-glass and water glass was broken and brass nails
forced out of the chairs

The nurse was knocked down and much injured by fire and splinters
but two persons standing next to her were unhurt

Mr Mantell at the street door his hair in a blaze

18th September 1852

Saturday morning

a tinner in Tor

Mr Pyle arose his usual hour

lighted the fire

went into the workshop

spoke to his apprentice

went to the privy

and fastening the door

suspended himself by the neck

with a handkerchief

from a staple over the door

sleeping in the open air for six weeks

February March 1912

John Harrison 53 years of age

on Monday evening in the Old Castle Inn

became faint

spilling some beer he'd been given

and between six and seven

the next morning was

found

lying further along Castle Road dead

near the track

leading across Bishop Down

4.30

Friday morning

6th January 1899

at the Dee Oil Works in Saltney

climbing a ladder carrying a naked lighted lamp

to the top of an oil still

leaking oil vapour ignited

and John Armstrong

was enveloped in flames

Friday 28th of December 1866 Robert Fey had been drinking

his wife found him at *The Hour Glass*

and for some time in Lime Kiln-lane they were heard quarrelling

Fey wished his wife to go home   she refused calling him foul
names and saying she would follow him wherever he went

he said if she did not go home he would knock her down and she
said *Do it! Do it!*

he struck her on the side of the head and she fell got up immediately
and walked to the door of her house close at hand crying

This is not the first time he has done it but it will be the last

when she got upstairs she was unconscious

she died four days later without recovering consciousness

Last scene of *The Revenge*

a tragedy

performed at the Liverpool Theatre

23 June 1804

Mr Barrymore in the role of *Alonzo*

struck himself violently with a dagger

wrested from the hand of

Mr Cooper in the role of *Zanga*

and fell upon the stage

calling softly for help   *I am wounded*

it is a real dagger   it was

a real African dagger a

favourite of Mr Cooper it

took a slanting direction across the lower ribs

and lodged in his belly blood

flowed over the stage

his body was found

in the water under the railway bridge

his watch stopped

at twenty minutes to seven

about the time of the high tide

when mistaking his way over the bridge

at Fremington Pill

Charles Pavey walked into the river

at the Deaf and Dumb Institution in Topsham-road   Monday

morning 22nd February 1897   just before half-past eight   and

immediately after breakfast

as the boys filed past through the teachers' dining-room   and up

the stairs to the dormitory to finish making their beds

                        sound of a fall

                lying on his side in a crouched position   on the

                lower landing of the stairs   a distance of 20 feet

                from the top   unconscious   his face covered with

                blood   a large swelling over the right temple and

                the right eye   Alfred James Currell aged 13 years

                son of an engine driver at Newton Abbot

alarmed by the smell of sheep-skins

piled high on the back of an ass

passing near the

horses of the New Lincoln coach

at Biggleswade

lifted their heads

breathed hard and furiously

set off with a sudden jerk

the coach-driver

dropping the reins fell

between the horses and the wheels

passed over him

killing him instantly

raising stones at Score Quarry

on the new road from Ilfracombe to Braunton

Thomas Moon aged 42

laid a train to blast some rock

retired at a proper distance

and after waiting some time

thinking the powder had not ignited

returning to see

his head was blown to atoms

melancholy occurrence

in Stepney a

bundle of

rags in a shop

doorway the

body of a

lad of fourteen or

fifteen years

quite dead

and cold

Anne Sweet aged fifteen

servant to Mr Trickey of Trull farm Whimple

had gone up to bed at ten a Saturday night

and having mended one of her stockings went down again to mend

the other

without a candle she thrust a couple of sticks into the embers on

the hearth

by their light she knelt to work

till overcome by fatigue she fell asleep

rushing up the stairs about half-past 12 she burst into her master's

bedroom her clothes all a-blaze of fire

screaming *Master don't 'e scold me don't 'e scold me*

      tinder from her clothes was found in the track of her flight at Bovey Farm in the parish of Beer and Seaton

Thursday 9th January 1838

a young woman named Susan Loaring

was found lying dead in the apple chamber

cotton shawl drawn tightly in a knot around her neck

I made sackcloth also my garment

under her shoulder a prayer book

opened to the 69th psalm

A sand bargeman

Henry Jones of Vauxhall

brought his barge down to the ballast engine off

Surrey-Street Strand

Monday morning about 4 o'clock August 20th 1834

making it fast he got into his boat

and his wife

jumping from the barge into his arms they were

thrown into the water

and sunk

together without trace

Monday 3rd January 1820

the niece of Mr Duff

dyer of East Smithfield

dreaming the house was on fire

woke from a deep sleep

shrieking

Fire! Fire!

he ran downstairs

poured a pail of water and

running back slipped

from the top of the stairs

falling to the bottom

breaking his neck

Saturday night after 11

James and Francis Cole furiously racing

two electric motor cars

eighteen or twenty miles an hour

past the Horse Guards up Whitehall

hitting a man called Leach

who stepped into the road

opposite the Shades public house

14th January 1899

Liverpool February 11th 1810

about quarter past ten the

bells of St. Nicholas were ringing

before divine service the congregation

beginning to gather in the yard

the keystone of the tower gave way

the spire bursting through the roof

with a crash along the central aisle

on children

from the charity school assembled

for their catechetical duties twenty-two bodies

were dragged from the ruins

Miss Helena Catherine Horn-Elphinstone-Dalrymple

aged 29 years daughter of

Sir Robert Graeme Horn-Elphinstone-Dalrymple Bart.

lately residing at 5 Alma Terrace in Kensington

paid a visit to Harrod's stores one Monday July 1909

and while her hair was being dressed

with tetra-chloride of carbon

became suddenly faint and died

mistaking it

for flour of sulphur

John and Thomas Bowen

at Walterstone

22 April 1780

took a large quantity of arsenic

in milk

to drive out the itch

The body of a youth named Cramp

bathing near the Summer House

at Teignmouth

opposite Coombe Cellars

was seized with cramp

his body

was picked up Wednesday morning

23rd of August 1876

by a lighterman below Hackney

11 years old she

drowned herself in a pool near her boarding school

Birmingham September 1816

and left her bonnet on the water's edge

pinned to it a letter

to her parents

intreating their forgiveness

and requesting for bearers

the young ladies she'd dreamed had carried her

to her grave

inclosing some locks of her hair

mementos of friendship

Jacob Feltham aged 73

labourer on one farm nearly

all his life

walked seven miles

from Chitterne

an October morning 1904

to apply for relief from

the Board of Guardians

at Warminster

granted 3s a week

he dropped dead

outside the workhouse door

leaving Moorgate at 12.40 a Wednesday afternoon

19th of December 1866

the Metropolitan Line down train to Kensington

passing the open area near Smithfield

workmen of the Thames Iron Company

swinging into position by the shear legs

a forty-foot cross girder of 40 tons

fell obliquely across the roof of the last carriage

sweeping through the compartments killing two men

and a widow of 66 named Johnson from Kennington

in her possession at the time of death

the sum of £200 in bank notes

concealed in secret pockets in her stays

George Thorne of Winterbourne Gunner was 76 years of age

for 69 years he worked on the same farm

he had a bad cold and cough but about 6.30 a late December
morning 1909 he started for his work walking to Porton Firs four
miles to pull turnips

he came home about 4.30 pm complaining of a pain in his chest

and after his tea he washed changed his clothes went into the
sitting-room and sat in the arm chair dozing

then struggling to breathe he died

100 feet above the water

John Thompson

a tailor half-drunk

acting for a wager

leaped from the high-level bridge at Sunderland

and was killed by concussion

Saturday May 17th 1823

Robert Baird aged 21 retired after supper to his bed-chamber

seated on the bed-side loading a large pistol

discharging its contents into his brain

a little beneath the right eye passing upwards behind the frontal

bone carrying off a large portion of the skull from the crown of his

head he fell back lifeless

on the bed

his garments were laid off as usual   bed-clothes folded down

Saturday night

a man and his wife

Blackfriars Road

quarrelling

she seized a brass candlestick

and threw it

missing him

it hit a woman

passing the street door at that moment

inflicting a severe head-wound

Monday 30th March 1896

Johanna Le Grass

died of syncope aged 44

shortly after giving birth

to her thirteenth child

stillborn

hoar frost on the rails

on the descent

from St Bees to Whitehaven

the 8 o'clock train from Ravenglass

Saturday morning 13th October 1849

hurtled through the S pieces through a yard wall

into a stone-built house carrying away

the kitchen a partition-wall

a girl of ten

among stones mortar smoke

John Whitton aged 77

found dead by his daughter

on her return from church

at Leyburn

sitting in his chair

book open on his knee

The Christian's Death

George Moore

a plumber aged 21 years

Thursday afternoon St James's Palace

bag of tools over his left shoulder

at the top of a ladder reaching

for the coping stone

to cross over from one roof to another

his hand slipped and he fell

forty feet onto rough stones

Harriet Salmon aged 16 years

Nursemaid to the Reverend Paton

at Tuddenham near Ipswich

escaped the vicarage by the window

a Wednesday night in January

taking with her an extra pair of boots

a supply of stockings an umbrella and her church service

leaving a letter in pencil

to another servant saying

her friends were to make no sorrow for her

and they would never see her

any more alive in this world she

had something on her mind

which caused her many miserable hours

since they had picked currants together

James Cane

mate of the *North Star*

now in the London Docks   October 18th 1862

walking from ward room to cabin

carrying a pair of scissors to trim a candle

tripped and fell on their point

piercing his jugular vein under the jawbone

5th April 1860 the mail steamers

left Queenstown for New York

with twenty-six country people

left stranded on board

saying goodbye to

friends and family of emigrants leaving

their carts and families behind at the dock

facing a journey of five thousand miles

to New York and back

on Sunday evening 2nd November 1834

in his barge under the arch of Cooney Bridge

on his passage to Bishop's Tawton

a lighterman Richard Parkhouse

oar coming in contact with the pier of the bridge

was thrown over the side

rose once and then sank

in the eddy which surrounds the bridge

and his body was not found

till past noon the following day

in the gut near the Black Rock

August evening a Thursday

standing in front of the saloon

of a shooting gallery in Dartmouth

Harry Forsey

hanging up glass bottles with a string to be shot at

was shot

in the back

from a rifle on a board

twelve or fourteen feet behind him

the owner of a lime-kiln

called Whitehead

one Sunday October 1802 at Wigmore

attempting to walk across the top of a

pit burning a few days the chalk

giving way beneath

he sunk down

and in a very short space was

burnt to a skeleton

between two and three in the afternoon

violent storms of thunder

hurricane and torrents of rain

the Strand in places a canal

Tuesday July 7th 1801

at the Westminster Court of Common Pleas

the wind drove rain against the skylight

with such violence the glass broke and a

torrent descended

on the wigs and cravats of Counsel

30th October 1859

Thomas Venturas aged 22

cook and steward aboard *The Curlew*

attached a grindstone to his neck

my life is no longer useful to any one

and jumped into the Bay of Biscay

lying on her side

bonnet on her head

for a month or six weeks

about 40 yards from the footpath

in a field of corn near the Old Gore Inn

the body of a young woman of twenty

putrid

dressed in linen gown white petticoat slippers

in her pocket two thimbles scissors some thread and needles

but no money

nobody missing in the neighbourhood

a stranger

Monday night nine o'clock

8 April 1844

The Fairy steamer from Greenwich

arriving at Old Shades Pier London Bridge

Mr. Foster the mate and money-collector

ticket-book in his hand

jumped and fell

between the wharf and the vessel

and drowned

An August evening 1851

son of one of the labourers

employed saving wheat on Solland Barton

parish of Sampford Courtenay

a little boy 10 years old

on the cart on a load of corn on its way to the rick

fell asleep

arriving at the rick yard in the dark

someone on the rick threw a pitch fork into the load

and into the boy's head

just above the ear

Frank Sanders

29 years of age

dancing master and member of the *Star Minstrel Troupe*

the morning he was to have been married at Paignton

Saturday 27 April 1895

was discovered on a bed in Exmouth dead

Bible and Prayer-book by his side

and a small bottle of oxalic acid empty

Joseph Connett painter and glazier forty-four years of age

26th December about half-past ten o'clock in the night

was found in the back yard of the Exeter Inn at Honiton

his leg broken just above the ankle

he said he was kicked in the leg by someone but

told his wife he slipped stepping on a piece of orange peel

and told the police he fell over a wheelbarrow

in the Devon and Exeter Hospital

suffered greatly from delirium tremens and could get no sleep

A light engine from Ipswich to Norwich

approaching Mellis station

around 35 miles per hour

10.20 a Monday morning 1883

Thomas Barker journeyman bricklayer of Diss aged 80

returning from the curate at Bargate with a basket of linen

at the gates of the foot-crossing

the signalman in his box warned him twice

not heeding or not hearing he crossed the down line

and was torn into pieces

fragments of his body scattered for yards around

were gathered up in a sack and

returned to his wife

waiting at home

Rev. Mr. Hopkinson

70 years of age

late curate of Byford

a gentleman of considerable property

on the 31st July 1823

at the cathedral church of Hereford

to marry a widow of 37

the solemn service proceeded

till the bridegroom took the ring out of his pocket

as she extended her hand suddenly

he fell back

and after a convulsive fit lasting a moment

lay on the ground a corpse

Richard Allen of Sourton

left his home for Sticklepath

crossing a portion of Dartmoor

to save three miles

was found dead from exposure and fatigue

the following afternoon

an umbrella under his feet

sitting under a rock near the Island of Rock

west of Okement river

whither he'd gone to shelter himself

during the boisterous night

a few minutes before ten

Saturday morning September 30th 1848

the nineteenth of twenty arches of the railway viaduct

crossing the Rother and the Beighton valley

fell in

immediately followed by thirteen or fourteen adjoining arches

and then the rest

burying four men one

was dug out alive

Sunday the 23rd of May 1852

farmer's son John Ware

went to evening service

at a Wesleyan Meeting-house in Topsham

after which he walked up towards Exeter

as far as the Country House Inn

and was not seen again

till eight days later his body was found

in the river near Clyst Bridge

2½ miles above Topsham

dressed as when he left home

with the exception of his hat and neckerchief

prayer book in one pocket

Bickersteith's hymns in another

a watch two keys one penny

A poorly clad woman was found

frozen to death

on the doorstep of a public house

at Neville's Cross near Durham

yesterday morning Wednesday

27th January 1897

a licensed victualler of Arthur Street in Chelsea

awakened by groans

and missing his wife from their bed

found her sitting on a chest in the dark

her cut throat bleeding profusely

by her side a razor covered with blood

between three and four o'clock

Sunday morning 18th December 1859

Thinking the 6.21 train from Liverpool-street

had stopped at Audley-end Station

a passenger named Pallett

opened the carriage door

stepped out

onto the coping of the bridge

learning his mistake too late as he

dropped seventy feet onto the roadway below

On Saturday evening

the body of a female infant was found

in the river Wye at Putson

sewed in a flannel envelope lined with coloured wool

mouth and throat full of ashes

Friday morning shortly before nine o'clock

third of April 1857

Thomas Scholefield

overlooker at George Brown & Co

manufacturers of Thornton-road Bradford

was replacing a belt turning horizontal shafts overhead

on the third storey of the mill

when he was whirled up

and round the shaft

head jammed against the drum

his back bent broken and twisted

his right arm torn off

Tuesday morning William Meadowcroft aged 28

engineman at Holt and Dent's dye-house

Isle of Cinder

Leeds

engaged in repairing a pipe

stooping down to pick up a tool he'd dropped

his clothes got entangled

and he was drawn by the revolving strap

to the top of the room

where the cog wheels and other gearing

broke his neck

and cut off one of his feet

five-year-old Hilda Dunford

was suddenly enveloped in flames

as she was passing along the pavement

in front of Milburn's garage

Marlborough High Street

a June morning

1911

Hartford Old Ironworks at Lower Moor

Monday morning half-past eight o'clock

the signal given for starting again after breakfast

three lads got on the hoist

raising themselves by pulling on the rope

one of them Ezekiel Astall aged 15

lying on the floor looked over the edge

as the cage reached the floor of the second storey

against which his head struck

and was completely severed from his body

loading stones from a quarry and leading the horse

Charles Brimley of Dean in Landkey

aged 11 years

returned home about six

a July evening

took a piece of bread and butter out into the yard

just returned with a cart-load of stones his brother

was standing by him

when he suddenly fell down dead

bread and butter in his hand

Hamilton 13th March 1820 a gentleman

firing at a dog in his garden the ball

broke a baker's window across the street

grazing the left side

of the head of his pregnant wife

Sunday afternoon

30th April 1820

a boy's dog with some difficulty

pulled out of a pond

in a field opposite the Eel Pie public-house in Limehouse

a large bundle

a flannel petticoat

the name *Bryson* in large letters

worked with a needle on it

and inside the body of an infant about a month old

a deep wound in the right side of his head

Turner the mason

of Stockland near Axminster

aged 71 in April 1896

died through drinking weed killer

in mistake for cider

from a stone jar

labelled *Poison*

St. James's Clerkenwell

31st July 1816

ten minutes past one o'clock a crash

as the boards shoring up a grave

West part of the burying ground

intended for Miss Burrows

fell in and the earth

closed over William Ruby

working eighteen feet down

Yesterday se'nnight

some men were attempting to back a waggon in Marden

a boy who was assisting

put his head between the spokes

trying to heave the wheel with his shoulders

the horses started forward

and the wheel going round

the boy's head was twisted against the bed of the wagon

and severed from his body

drunk Christmas Day 1899

and Boxing Day

taken to the General Hospital

John Jordan a shepherd of Tettenhall Wood

told the house surgeon he'd taken medicine

for foot-rot in sheep

and died of mercury poisoning

Frances Hill

between three and four on a Sunday morning

1st April 1832

climbed up a lamp iron in Brydges-street

and broke the glass of the gas lamp

to light a cigar

Sunday 21st July 1844

a labouring man named Bartlett

went to the Lime Kiln near Branscombe

to dress some potatoes

found a foot and a half from the edge of the kiln

quite burnt

beside a small pitcher with some gooseberries in it

and his corpse

face and upper body destroyed by fire

Mr Potowski an Italian

one Thursday evening in April

1832

passing along Holborn with a board on his head

on which were busts of celebrated characters

Paganini Fox Pitt Wellington O'Connell &c.

images in plaster of Paris

James Murphy had been drinking

ran purposely into him

knocking his stock to the ground

fragments strewed in all directions

She nodded over a prayer book

and the candle caught her locks a

quantity of beautiful curls

in a blaze

William Pyke aged forty-seven

a thatcher by trade

was at the Buller's Arms in Exwick

drinking cider for three or four hours

leaving about 9.30 in the evening

neither drunk nor sober

several weeks later his body was found

in the river Exe

hanging to a bush

in his pockets 7s. 11 ¼d

keys a knife and a watch

stopped at twenty-six minutes to eleven

on his way home

from Mr Wreyford's

at Dockham where he'd gone

to get ferrets to clear a house of vermin

John Guy

left Taverner's public-house intoxicated

between two and three Saturday afternoon

9th January 1841

and was found days later on Mardon-down

lying on one side

in a crooked position

frozen to the ground

Joseph Lewis servant to Mrs. Bennett

of Nethertown in the parish of Pencoyd

brought a bull to Hereford fair

and drove it back

at the fold gate

the animal suddenly attacked

and so injured him he died in a few minutes

the bull was immediately shot

by order of Mrs. Bennett who

distributed the meat to the poor of the parish

Timothy Collins a boy of fourteen

I am a shoeblack

and was in Crooked Lane on Monday with my box

when the prisoner

standing at the bar shaking and shivering

coat and trousers hung about him in tatters

secured to his waist by a rope

came up and asked me to black his shoes I told him

there was so much mud on 'em they wouldn't shine

and so I'd rather not do 'em

with that he ups with his foot and kicks me over

and when I was on the ground

he kicks me five or six times more

a gentleman unknown

about fifty-five years of age

died suddenly at the railway station in Richmond

Tuesday 27th April 1852

on his person a letter

relating to the ship *Thames*

addressed from Richmond Street

signed *Samuel Shipton*

one Tuesday George Gray aged about eight years went turfing on the
moor near Sheepstor
with another lad about 16 years old

after working about three hours the elder boy left him by the side of
the turf rick to go to two men employed on another rick quarter of
a mile distant

near the child were two horses grazing

it was raining very hard the mist was driving strongly and very thick
and returning to the spot they could find neither child nor horses

the father and others traversed the moor with lanterns all night
without success

on the following day the two horses were found in the fens but
though twenty persons searched the moor the whole of Wednesday
the boy was not found

until Thursday morning lying on his breast dead on the moor on
the ground several miles from the spot where he had been at work

It was raining fast

and the wind was blowing a gale

and passing under a bridge

a mile and three quarters east of Halwill Junction

John Cleverly a telegraph labourer

was blown against the engine of the 12.05 p.m. train

from Okehampton

fell under the wheels

and was cut in two

Tuesday noon 6th January 1789

three men walked over the ice

across the Thames

from Execution Dock to the opposite shore

     and a girl of the town

     about eighteen was found

     frozen to death in an alley

     near Stratton-ground Westminster

A sailor from a vessel near Hermitage-stairs

getting a bucket of water

at a hole made in the ice

slipped

and fell in

and disappeared though his cries were heard

as he was carried away by the current

invisible beneath the ice

a large masted vessel

with a cargo of American pine

drifting towards the Brannaghs

an uninhabited island within a mile of Arran

struck

and immediately went to pieces

no crew no papers and her name

where she was sailing from

or her destination

unknown

Monday evening about eight o'clock

one of the horses drawing a bus

eastwards up Ludgate-hill

became restive

breaking his hoof through one of the windows

a single flying splinter

cut the face of Harriet Harding

At Pontecraft

Thursday 18th December 1835

a boy aged 14

apprentice to Mr Bevitt ironmonger

working on a pump in a well 23 yards deep

holding a candle

and looking up to the well mouth

a pair of smith's iron tongs fell from the top

penetrated the boy's cap and his skull above the eyebrows

passing through the eye socket and the palate

through muscles and skin

appearing three inches below the under jaw

touching the sternum

a body seen floating

with the coming tide

outside the Quay

at Barnstaple

Monday 9th October

was brought to shore

Found Drowned

and identified

as Thomas Fraser

aged 10 years missing

since Friday

September the 29th

Between two and three

a Thursday afternoon in January

Mrs Caroline Pattison

widow of Devonshire Street Portland-place

two doors from her house

stepped on a slide and fell backwards

striking the back of her head against the stone coping

of the area railing

blood gushing from her nose and ears

dark hair

five feet seven inches in height

of slender make

of very extraordinary quiet harmless and inoffensive habits

John Davis aged twenty

employed for three years

by a picture dealer and frame maker on Fleet Street

Monday 5th January 1835

around seven in the morning

was sent by his master to Tower-stairs

to inquire about the arrival of a steam vessel from Antwerp

and was never seen again

on Tuesday afternoon about five

a young man looking like a farmer

mounted on a spirited blood horse

rode up to the shop of Mr. Stray

tailor and draper on Salthouse-lane in Hull

helped himself to a pair of trousers hanging at the window

and rode off

Thursday 29th March 1832

L'Actif a French brig

from St Domingo bound for Le Havre

with 150 tons of mahogany

was found off the Lizard in a state of wreck

water-logged

masts gone

and no crew

John George Hannaford aged 25

left the Bolton Hotel in Brixham

in a cab about 10.30 a.m.

taking a double-barrelled gun

and arriving near to the lodge of Lord Churston's residence

shot himself in the mouth

a piece of paper in his pocket

Good-bye forever

the only words decipherable

and forty mourning cards

for his mother who is not dead

Richard Stacey aged 16

of Brook Street in Kensington

walking under scaffolding in Fitzroy Square

Thursday morning 17th October 1867

a large plank dropped on his head

fracturing his skull

killing him instantly

Mrs Susanna Davey landlady of the *Ring of Bells*

Worcester Street Plymouth

a widow 68 years of age

took out a white dress trimmed with lace in which she desired she

might be buried and requested her servant to air it before the fire

she left in perfect health for Church

passing through the church-yard to the graves of her husband and

her sister

taken suddenly ill   the dress was lying on a chair when she was

brought back into her house

until two o'clock in the afternoon Sunday 20 January 1839 she

departed this life

Walking through Greenwich Park

reading a newspaper

on the edge of the path a man named Sadler

was injured by deer

remarkably tame

accustomed to be fed from paper bags

and died

at the college farm of the Express Dairy Company

on Regents Park Road

a dairy hand was found lying

dead of a bullet wound killed

by a stray shot the tragedy

was an accident

Alice Westcott aged nineteen had taken down the candlesticks and other articles from the mantelpiece to be cleaned

and amongst the rest was a fowling piece which had not been taken down for several months and which she placed on a table near the fire place

where a little boy of the name of Warren began to play with it unobserved

and loaded it went off

through her cheek and into her head

sent by his mother to purchase a little tobacco

to take to his father

a blacksmith at work in the mines

Aaron Hayman four years of age

was not missed until evening

when his cap was seen floating

on the pond adjoining the counting-house

last night

at the Novelty Theatre in Great Queen Street

during *Sins of the Night*

the final scene as

Wilfred Moritz Franks stabbed Temple E. Crozier

the spring of the trick dagger failed to act

and the weapon pierced the actor's heart

who died as the curtain was lowered

Jane Bell widow of a navy surgeon who died about 18 months since was intoxicated every day

and talked wildly her house was all on fire she had nothing but devils about her

she bought a sheet of paper to write to her sister in Falmouth and ask her to come up for

she was very unwell

it was afterwards found with the words   *Devonport. Dear Sister, I have taken*

on Monday 22nd October 1849 she was found

dead in her house in Andrew's-lane in an upstairs room in bed partially undressed with a bottle marked morphia and a jug containing beer

articles of furniture were in a confused state the staircase strewed with clothes in the garret were a quantity of ladies' dresses and under her pillow was a valuable gold watch and guard-chain

27th July 1869

Rev. Julius Elliott on the Shreckhorn

today I begin to live again

springing from snow onto rocks

a thin glaze of ice

slipped

and fell

gliding rapidly down the steep snow slope

rolling occasionally

until he disappeared from sight

near the Lauter-aar glacier

a thousand feet below

about midnight his horse returned home without his rider

saddle upon his back but no bridle

next morning the body of Thomas Parminter of Brightleycot

was found in New Barn Wood near Youlston Old Park

lying on the ground like a person asleep

he had taken off his coat

carefully folded it up and placed it under his head as a pillow

his hat was drawn over his eyes

as if to protect him from the sun

his neck-cloth was loosened as also his waistcoat

left hand resting on his chest

Saturday night after ten o'clock

Ellen Vinmore

under the influence of liquor

near the kerb in Cheapside

opposite the giants striking Bennett's clock

a man walking towards St. Paul's her husband

put his hands on her shoulders

and pushed her she

fell into the roadway

an omnibus passed over her right foot

was amputated she

died

Four o'clock in the afternoon

five children walking home from school

through Crowfield to Pettaugh into drifting snow

a dog rushed at them barking

and the frightened children scattered

Kate Willis aged six ran into the road

where she was knocked down by four horses

and the wheels of the cart

full of sacks of coke and coal

ran over her

as the Torquay train came into Newton station

Friday evening at nine o'clock

going about five miles an hour

the guard James Hobbs

attempting to reach the ground

holding on by the handle

ran a few yards with the train

the step caught his leg

spun him round he fell on his back

legs thrown into the air

and the left one

caught the last wheel of the van

which went over him

The Stag mail steamer

on her passage from Glasgow to Belfast

March 1857

twenty cabin passengers and seventy-two in steerage

in a dense snow-storm heading at half-speed

early Sunday morning ran ashore

we have struck

on a low rocky promontory near Blackhead

snow falling very thick

the vessel fast filling and sinking at the bow

sea pouring into the steerage cabin

by the light of the compass-box

a woman reading her prayer-book or bible

distress rockets shooting into the night

on his way home from Rotterdam to Leith on the steamer *Holyrood*

a gentleman of Coupar-Angus enclosed his card in a bottle

pencilling on the back he would pay a sum to anybody who delivered

this card to his address

and dropped it carefully corked into the sea 9th September 1865 at

noon about 100 miles from the mouth of the Rhine

and around three o'clock on the afternoon of October the 5th a fisher-

man picked up the bottle on the Suffolk shore above Sizewell Gap

Wednesday evening July 26th 1849

The Nassau balloon

seven persons in the car and four on the hoop

rose above the Vauxhall Gardens

and took a south-westerly direction

suddenly rocking to and fro over Westminster-road

dropping within a few feet of the housetops

barely missing chimney tops

reeling down Gaywood-street to the London-road

heaving first one way then the other

it struck No.94

tearing down brickwork and part of the chimney stack

throwing three men on the hoop onto the house-top

then ascended towards Bromley

and was quickly out of sight

in any event at all events

a certain place a

particular interval of time   occurrence

incident episode   bare instant

regardless of circumstances in any case

in the event of   in case of

if in the event of

that if it should happen

any day now that

in which case

no matter how many or how few

even the smallest amount or

even one no matter

how much or how little

to any degree or extent   at all

on the railway it was

dark and the moon

gave no light on the

track or the body

lying in the four-foot way

near Skew Bridge nothing

to identify him

aged between fifty and sixty

Lightning Source UK Ltd.
Milton Keynes UK
UKHW01f0606210518
322897UK00001B/9/P